Abstract Geometric Shapes & Painted Moments

ADULT COLORING BOOK WITH POETRY AND SELF-DISCOVERY

Aventuras De Viaje

Copyright SF Nonfiction Books © 2024

All Rights Reserved

No part of this document may be reproduced without written consent from the author.

www.SFNonfictionBooks.com

INTRODUCTION

Welcome to the captivating universe where geometry merges with artistry, where the precision of abstract shapes intertwines with the fluidity of painted moments. This book is not merely a collection—it's an exploration, a meditation, and a celebration of the intricate dance between structured forms and spontaneous expressions.

Each page invites you deeper into a world of bold geometric configurations and vibrant color palettes, where sharp angles and soft curves form a visual symphony of self-discovery. These designs, symbols of clarity, creativity, and personal insight, await your interaction to truly come alive. Engaging with these elements offers not just a visual feast but also a profound connection with the core of your artistic spirit.

In the rush of our daily routines, the opportunity to pause and delve into our inner landscapes is priceless. This book encourages you to slow down, to immerse yourself in a realm of artistic precision and poetic reflection, and to reconnect with the harmonious pulse of your personal journey. It's a chance to ignite your imagination and fill it with the colors of introspection and discovery.

Embark on this creative expedition, navigating through the layers of geometric abstraction and the emotive power of poetry. Here, you're not just observing; you're interacting with art, unleashing your creativity, and experiencing the tranquility of artistic mindfulness.

Discovering the Mosaic of Imagination

Dive deeper, and you'll find that this book has been meticulously crafted to enhance your personal journey:

- **Simple Activities:** Beyond just coloring, engage with activities designed to spark reflection and creativity. These gentle prompts will lead you to moments of introspection, serving as kindling for your inner fire.

- **Quotes:** Let the wisdom of personal development accompany you, illuminating your path as you add your own burst of color to the pages.

- **Positive Affirmations:** As you color, let these words of positivity uplift your spirit, molding your thoughts and inspiring a brighter perspective.

- **Poems and Haikus**: Delight in the poetic tales that complement the theme of this book, capturing life's varied rhythms and experiences. Each verse and every line serve as a muse for your artistic endeavors, enhancing your coloring journey with lyrical inspiration.

Embark on this coloring odyssey, immersing yourself in a world of diverse themes and the therapeutic embrace of art. Each page invites you on a unique journey, blending your creativity with the tranquility of coloring.

THANKS FOR YOUR PURCHASE

Get Your Next SF Nonfiction Book FREE!

Claim the book of your choice at:

www.SFNonfictionBooks.com/Free-Book

You will also be among the first to know of all the latest releases, discount offers, bonus content, and more.

Go to:

www.SFNonfictionBooks.com/Free-Book

Thanks again for your support.

**Daily Blessing:
What made you smile today?**

_____

_____

"In the geometry of life, every angle you choose can illuminate a different path."

I embrace my creativity and paint my journey with bold colors.

In lines and colors, A hidden symmetry speaks— Life's complex patterns.

Creative Spark: Describe a color that matches your mood today.

_____

_____

"Creativity is not about painting life; it's about creating your life as a masterpiece."
— John C. Maxwell

I am a masterpiece in progress, constantly evolving and growing.

Shapes merge and divide,
Life's mosaic, colorful,
Infinite designs.

Geometric Insight:
Which shape do you feel like today and why?

_____

_____

"Each color you choose paints a new chapter in the book of your journey."

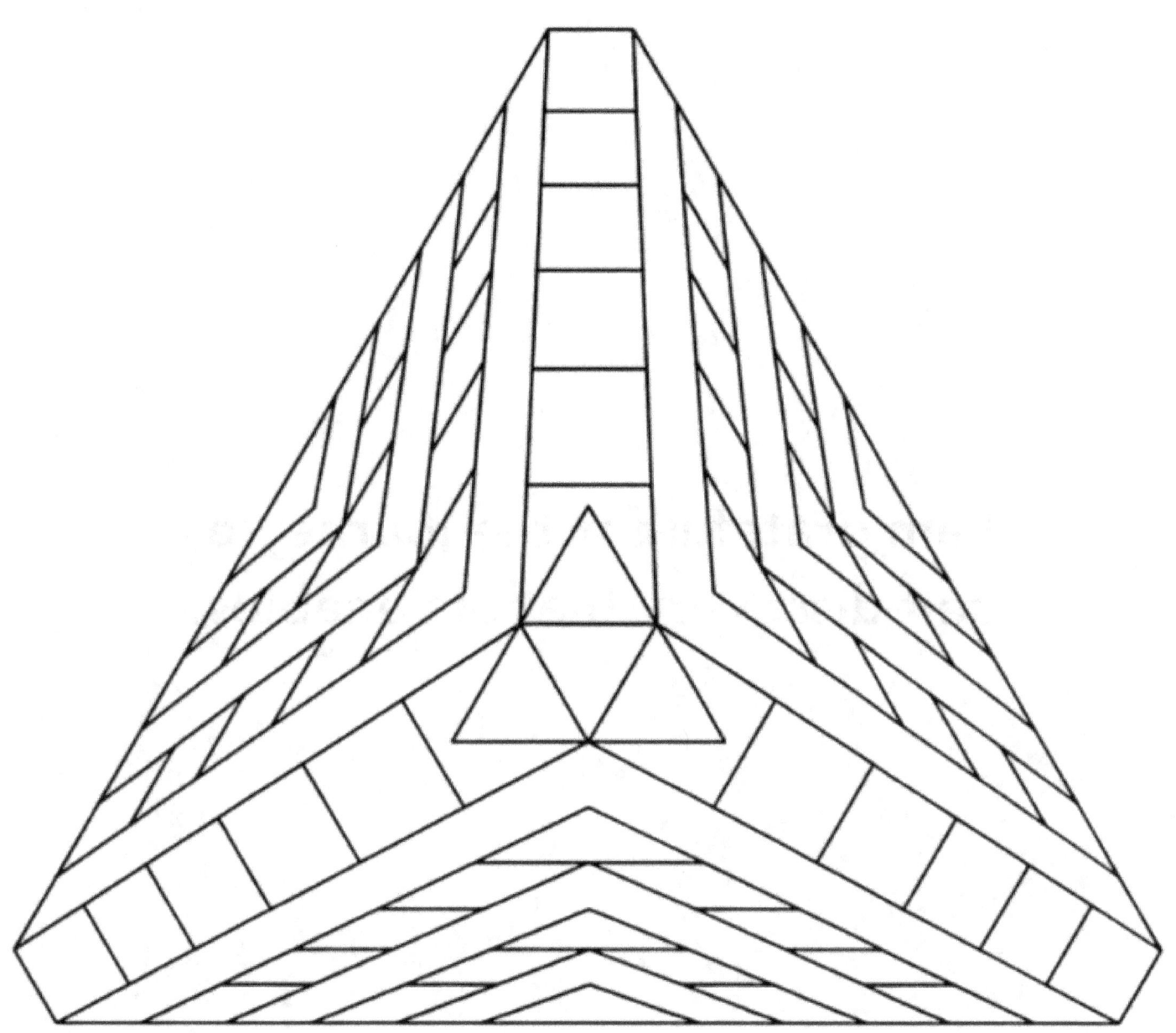

I am grateful for the journey of self-discovery that art enables.

With every stroke drawn, New paths in the maze of mind, Discoveries bloom.

Poetry Pause:
Write a four-line poem about this moment.

_____

_____

The mind is like a parachute; it works best when open."
— Frank Zappa

I celebrate my unique perspective and express it freely.

Bold lines curve and twist,
Thoughts unfurl like spiral stairs,
Climbing to new heights.

Kindness Canvas:
Who did you help today and how did it make you feel?

_____

_____

"Self-discovery is not a straight line—it's a spiral of continuous growth."

I am connected to my inner wisdom through every line I draw.

Shadows and light play,
On the canvas of our souls,
Painting who we are.

Gratitude Geometry:
Name three things in your life that have many angles but bring you joy.

_____

_____

"The greatest masterpiece is your life's story."

I am confident in my ability to create beauty in my life.

Geometric dawn,
Sunlight splits the horizon,
Day breaks into shapes.

Positive Polygon:
Draw a shape that represents your aspiration for tomorrow.

_____

_____

"Embrace the complexity of your inner geometry; every shape holds a story."

I am a channel of creativity,
flowing with ideas and inspirations.

In the heart of shapes,
The essence of you and me,
Mirrored perfectly.

Tranquil Triangles:
List three peaceful moments from your day.

_____

_____

"Paint your life with bold colors and brave strokes."

— Henri Matisse

I am reflective, learning from every pattern I create and encounter.

Circles intertwine,
Like our lives, endlessly looped,
Eternal, complete.

Reflective Symmetry:
What balance did you find in your life today?

_____

_____

"The only journey is the journey within."
— Rainer Maria Rilke

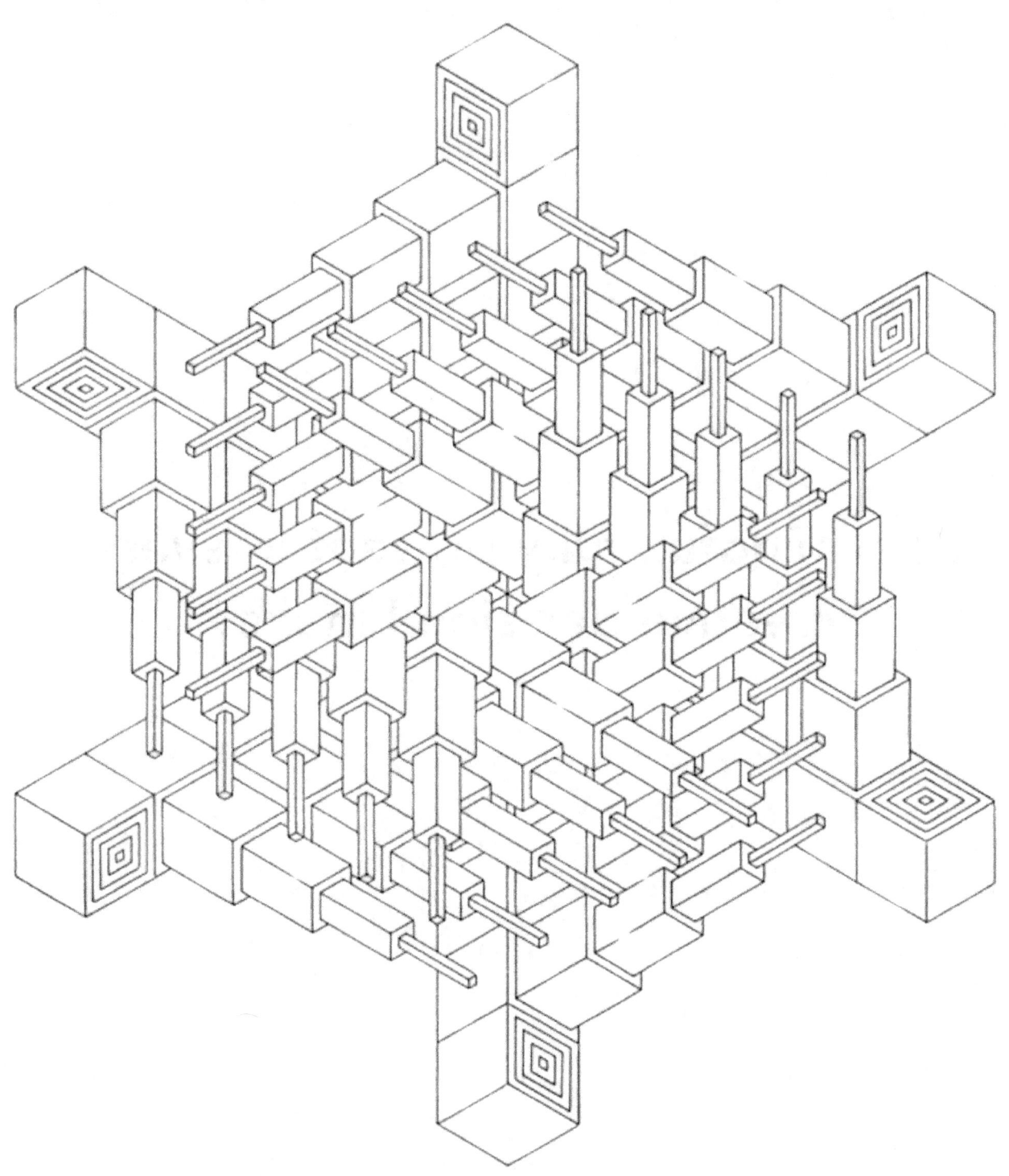

I am mindful, fully present in every creative decision I make.

Beneath the surface, Complex patterns of the heart, Waiting to be seen.

Self-Discovery Space:
What did you learn about yourself while coloring today?

_____

_____

"Art is a line around your thoughts."
— Gustav Klimt

I am resilient, adapting and thriving with every challenge.

Beneath the surface,
Complex patterns of the heart,
Waiting to be seen.

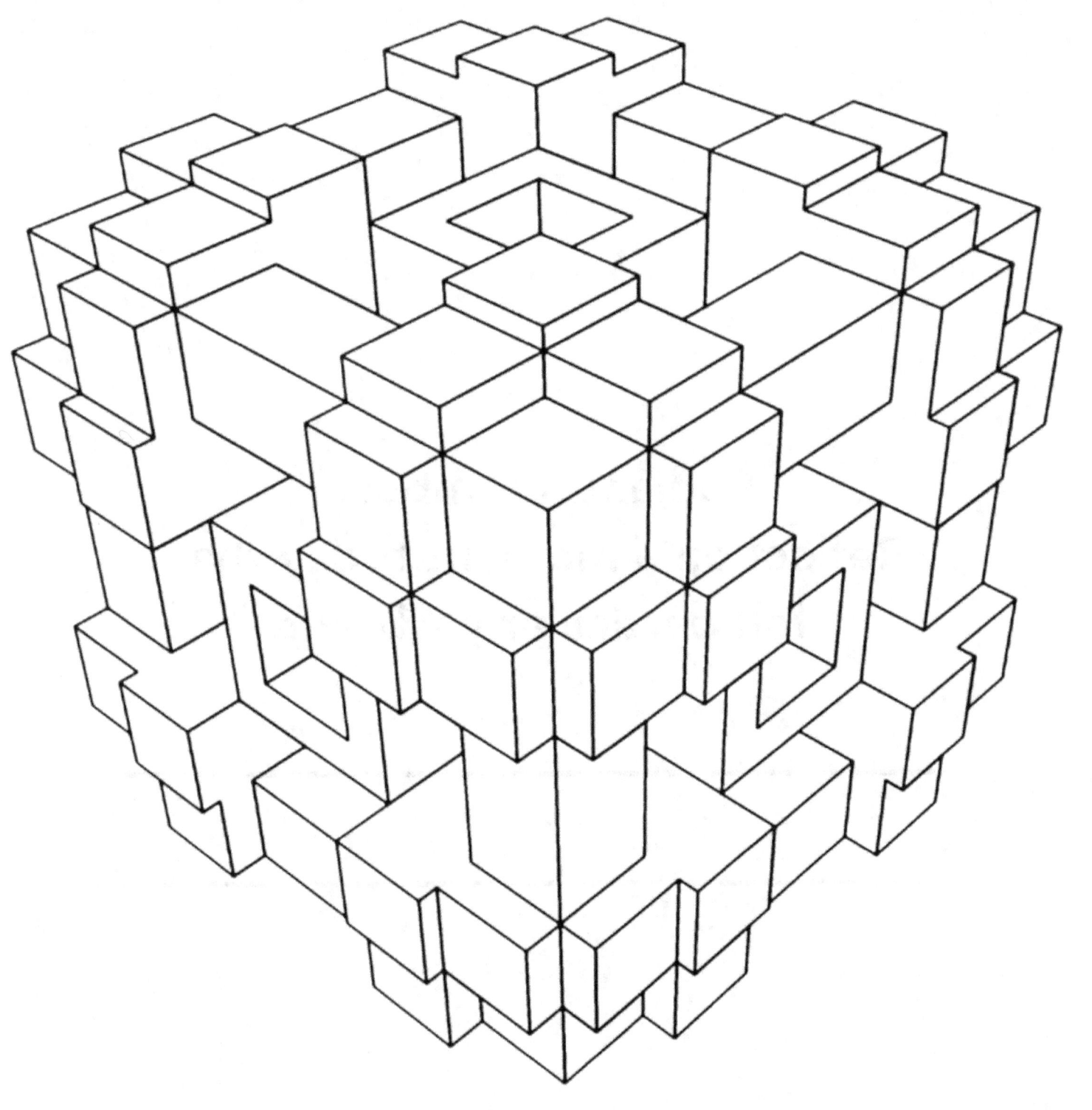

**Radiant Rhombus:
Reflect on a moment today that felt particularly vibrant.**

_____

_____

"Every moment is a fresh beginning."

— T.S. Eliot

I am deserving of a peaceful and creative life.

Triangles point paths,
Directions for the seeker,
Sharp turns to wisdom.

Artistic Adventure:
How was today an adventure in art and self-expression?

_____

_____

"Harmony and chaos are colors in the palette of life."

I am bold, not afraid to use vibrant colors and unique patterns.

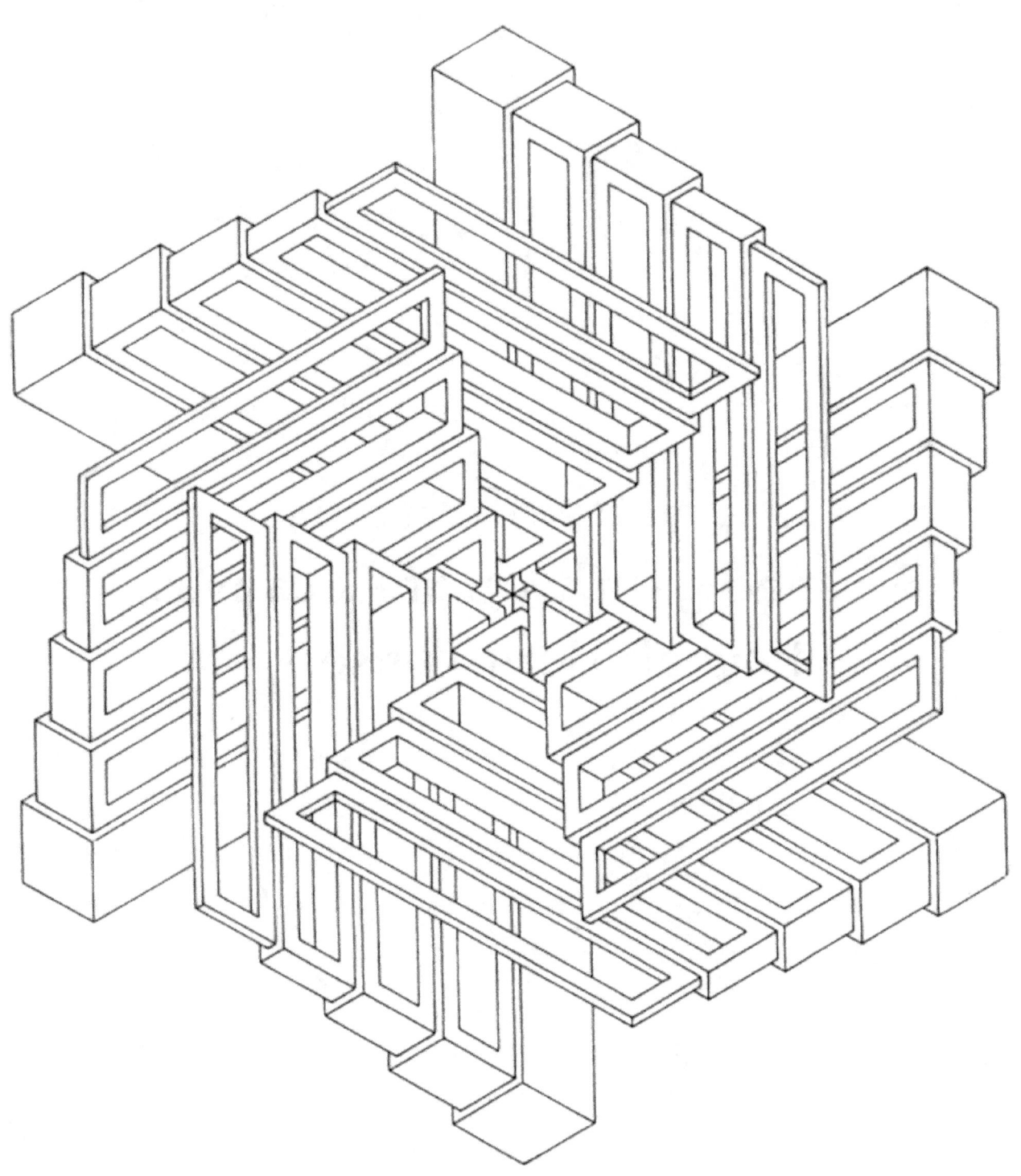

A palette of dreams,
Brushed gently on life's canvas,
Reveals depth unseen.

Affirmation of Alignment:
Align your intentions with your actions.

_____

_____

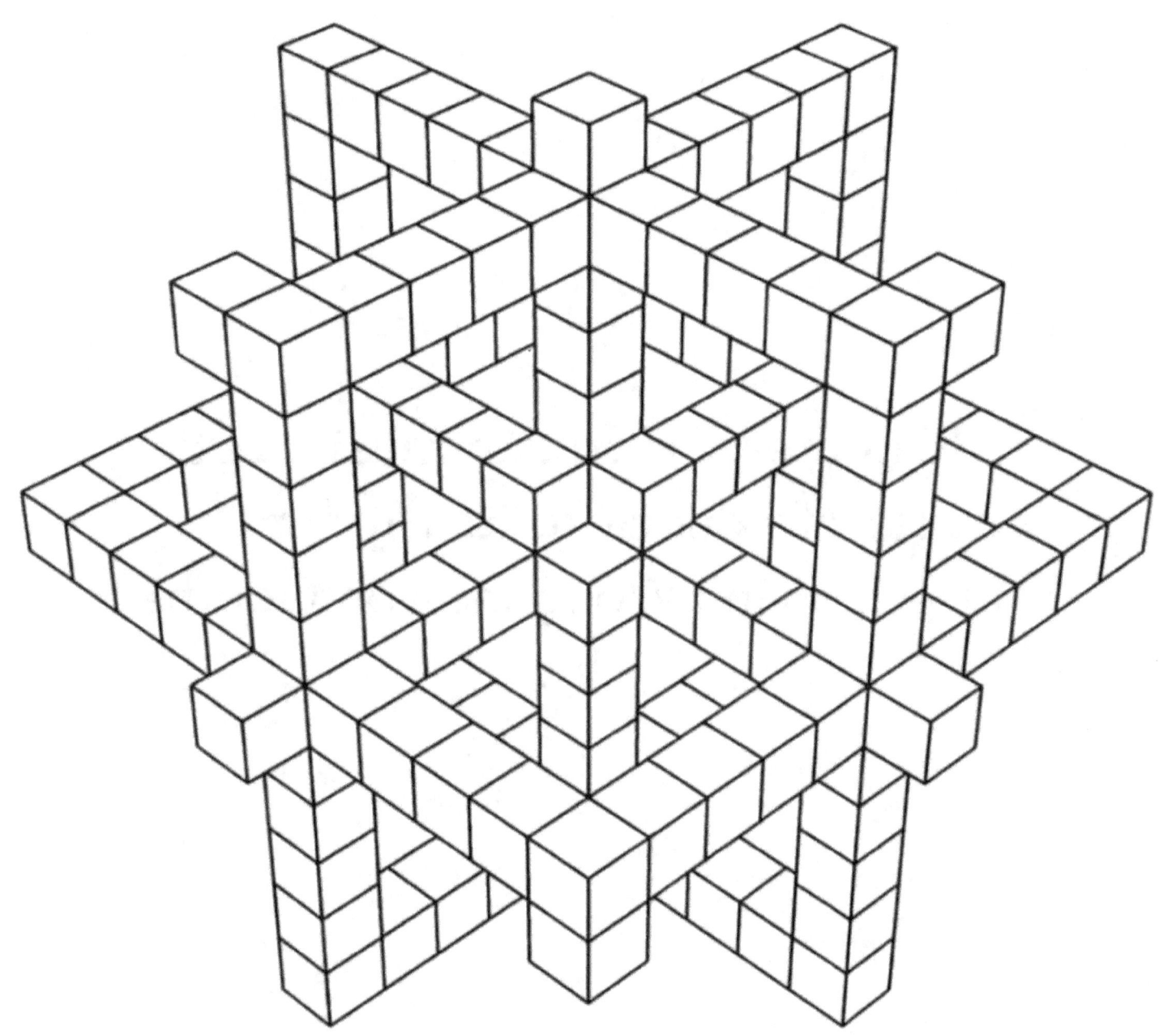

"Geometry is frozen music. Let your life dance to its rhythm."
— Johann Wolfgang von Goethe

BEYOND THESE PAGES

A Deeper Dive into Art and Soul Awaits!

This book is but a chapter in a voyage where creativity meets depth.

Craving more? Explore the link below and weave deeper into the tapestry of art and emotion.

www.SFNonfictionBooks.com/Adult-Coloring-Books

A HEARTFELT THANK YOU

As the colors on these pages have come to life, so has our shared journey in this artistic realm. I am deeply grateful for your trust in choosing this book, and more so for allowing it to be a part of your self-care and personal journey.

Taking time for oneself is a gift—a silent promise of growth, introspection, and rejuvenation. By picking up the colors and filling these pages, you've not just created art but have also woven moments of peace, reflection, and creativity into your life.

Thank you for making space for yourself, for embracing the wonders within these pages, and for dancing to the rhythm of the lines and hues within this book. Your journey here is a testament to the beauty of dedicating time to one's soul and spirit.

If you enjoyed this journey and wish to explore more, know that there are other themes awaiting your artistic touch. Dive into new worlds and let your imagination flow.

From the deepest corner of my heart, thank you for bringing this book to life. Until our next artistic adventure together, cherish the colors of your journey and continue to shine.

Warmly,

Aventuras De Viaje

ABOUT THE AUTHOR

Aventuras has three passions: travel, writing, and learning new skills.

Combining these three things, Miss Viaje spends her time exploring the world and learning about anything and everything that interests her, from yoga, to music, to science, and more.

Aventuras takes what she discovers and shares it through her books.

www.SFNonfictionBooks.com

www.ingramcontent.com/pod-product-compliance
Lightning Source LLC
Chambersburg PA
CBHW081621100526
44590CB00021B/3540